A First Book of Mozart

For The Beginning Pianist

with Downloadable MP3s

Introduction

Meet Wolfgang Amadeus Mozart, one of the greatest music creators in history. His music is famous all over the world, and in this book, "A First Book of Mozart: For Beginners on the Piano," we'll help you learn to play his amazing songs.

Mozart was a musical genius. He wrote his first piece when he was just eight years old! Now, we want to share his beautiful music with you, even if you're just starting to play the piano.

This book is like a special guide that will show you how to play Mozart's music. You'll find some of his most famous songs here, made easy for beginners. From cheerful dances to fun tunes, we've chosen music that's fun and not too hard to play. It's your ticket to start enjoying Mozart's magical world of music on the piano!

But there's more! We've included sheet music and downloadable MP3s for some of Mozart's most famous compositions, such as the haunting "Fantasia in D minor," the beautiful "Piano Sonata No. 11," the mesmerizing "Requiem Piano Mozart," the joyful "Allegretto from Piano Concerto No. 17," and the intricate "Mozart 12 Variations on a French Nursery." These downloads will help you learn and play these masterpieces with confidence, all from the comfort of your piano. It's like having Mozart himself as your teacher! So, let's embark on this musical adventure together and dive into the world of Mozart's timeless melodies.

Allegretto from Piano Concerto No.17

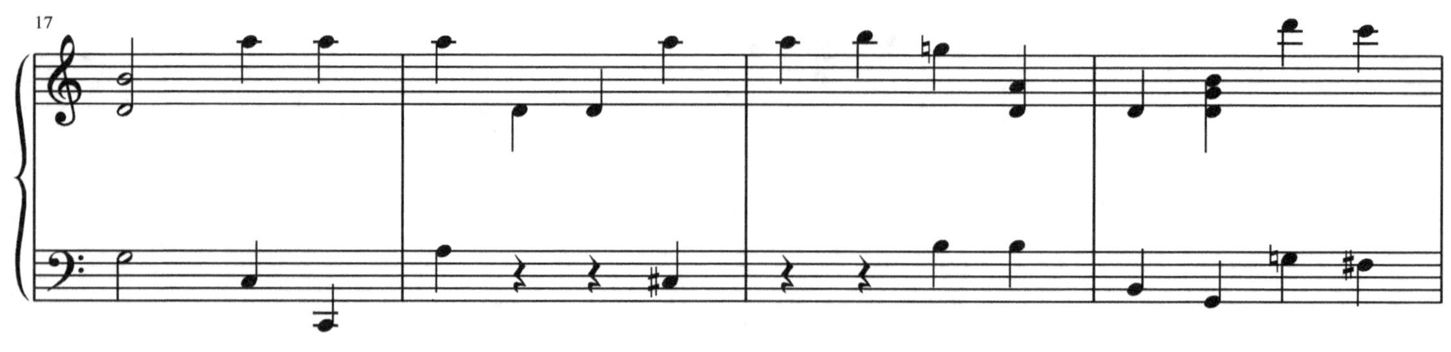

PHANTASIE N.º 3
für das Pianoforte
von
W. A. MOZART.
Köch. Verz. N.º 397.

Mozarts Werke.

Serie 20. N.º 20.

Ausgegeben 1873.

cresc.
f p
cresc.
f
p
cresc. f
Presto.
Tempo I.
f
p
f
p
f p
cresc. -
cresc. -
f
f p
cresc. -
f

Presto.
Tempo I.
p
p
f
fp
f
p
Allegretto.
dolce
p
1.

2.
legato
legato
f
a tempo
rallent.
dolce
f
p
f
p
pp
p
f
ff

12 VARIATIONEN
über „Ah vous dirais-je, Maman"
für das Pianoforte
von
W. A. MOZART.
Köch.Verz. № 265.

VAR. II.
legato
VAR. III.
tr
f

VAR. IV.
VAR. V.
p

VAR.VI.
2/4
p
legato
cresc.
f
p legato
cresc.
f
p
cresc.
f
f

VAR. VII.
VAR. VIII.
Minore.
f
p
f
p
f
f

VAR. IX.
Maggiore.

8(42)
VAR. XI.
Adagio.
p
fp
fp
cresc.
sf
p
3
3
sf
sf
VAR. XII.
Allegro.
tr
tr
tr
f
tr
tr
W. A. M. 265.

SONATA IX.

Abbreviations: P.T., Principal Theme; S.T., Sec- | Abkürzungen: HS. bedeutet Hauptsatz, SS. Seiten-
ondary Theme. | satz.

Tema.

Andante grazioso. (♪ = 120.)

Var. I.

a) *mp* (*mezzo piano*, rather soft,) viz., between *p* and *mf*.

a) *mp* (*mezzo piano*, ziemlich schwach) bedeutet einen Grad von Tonstärke, welcher zwischen *p* und *mf* steht.

a) easier: / leichter:

b) **Strike these appoggiaturas exactly on the beat.**

b) Die Vorschlagsnote mit dem *cis* oben gleichzeitig anschlagen, und so fort.

c) easier: / leichter:

p
cresc.
f
Var. III. (♪ = 112.)
p
f
sempre legato.

mp
p
f
fz
a)
Var. IV. (♪=120.)
m.g.
p
f
mp
mf
p
a)

Var. V.
Adagio.(♪= 60.)
cresc.
f
p
f
p
p
f
p
f
p
p
cresc.
dim.
1.
2.
a)
b)
a)
b)

a)   b)   c) See **a**), previous page.
c) Wie **a**) auf voriger Seite.

d) Begin the embellishment with the bassnote *a*, and execute it so quickly, that the principal note *c* sharp, is struck before the entrance of the *c* sharp in the bass.

Den Vorschlag mit dem *a* im Basse zu beginnen, jedoch so schnell auszuführen, dass die Hauptnote *cis* noch vor dem *cis* des Basses eintritt.

a) Make these appoggiaturas very short, but distinct; strike them exactly on the beat.

b) The *c* sharp must enter with the fundamental note of the left hand. All the broken chords in this variation are very emphatic.

c)

d) Both hands begin and end together.

a) Diese Vorschläge auf den Anfang des Takttheils, sehr kurz aber deutlich.

b) Mit der Grundnote der linken Hand muss das *cis* in der rechten Hand eintreten. Alle gebrochenen Accorde in dieser Variation sehr markirt.

c)

d) Beide Hände zusammen anfangen und aufhören.

a) Play the first note of the embellishment with the bass.

a) Die erste Vorschlagsnote tritt gleichzeitig mit dem Bass ein.

a)

b) This trill is undoubtedly intended to end with the following figure in thirty second notes, instead of the usual turn: . But the customary close is easier, and is allowable:

b) Dieser Triller ist wohl ohne den gewöhnlichen Nachschlag von unten beabsichtigt, indem die folgenden Zweiunddreissigstel die Stelle des letzteren vertreten: Zur Erleichterung mag jedoch folgende Ausführung gewählt werden:

a) The appoggiaturas on the beats.   a) Die Vorschläge auf den Anfang des Takttheils.

f
mf
p
mf
p
mp
cresc.
p
f
dim.
p
5
3
f
mf
f
1.
2.
Menuetto D.C.

Rondo

Alla Turca
Allegretto (♩ = 126)

W. A. MOZART

a) Always begin the embellishment on the beat.

b)

c) Play the bass with the c sharp in the right hand, accent it strongly, and so proceed throughout the entire theme.

a) Den Vorschlag immer mit dem Takttheil beginnen.

c) Der Bass muss mit dem cis der rechten Hand gleichzeitig eintreten und sehr markirt gespielt werden, auf gleiche Weise durch den ganzen Satz.

P.T. HS.
p
mp
p
cresc.
fz p
tr
S.T. SS.
f
1.
2.
CODA.

a) Sustain the half note c sharp, but otherwise play the chords alike in both hands. Let the hands begin exactly together, and attack the highest note together.

b)

c) The appoggiaturas as at b.

a) Die Ausführung in der rechten Hand ist wie in der linken Hand, nur dass die halbe Note cis gehalten wird; rechte und linke Hand muss gleichzeitig beginnen und gleichzeitig auf dem obersten Ton eintreffen.

b)

c) Ausführung des Vorschlags wie bei b.

Requiem Piano Mozart

NMA I / 1 / Abt. 2 / 2: KV 626 / 10

N⁰ 2 Hostias

⟨Mozart und Süßmayr⟩

*) Bezifferung im Hostias nach dem Stimmenerstdruck; vgl. Vorwort, S. XX, und Krit. Bericht

138

*) Takt 9, Fagott II, Vokal- und Instrumentalbaß, letzte Note: Süßmayr schreibt B.
**) Takt 9, Viola, letzte Note: Süßmayr schreibt as.

ho - sti - as et pre - ces ti - bi Do - mi - ne
ho - sti - as et pre - ces ti - bi Do - mi - ne
ho - sti - as et pre - ces ti - bi Do - mi - ne
ho - sti - as et pre - ces ti - bi Do - mi - ne
Tutti
lau - dis of - fe - ri - mus: tu su - sci - pe pro a - ni - ma - bus il - lis,
lau - dis of - fe - ri - mus: tu su - sci - pe pro a - ni - ma - bus il - lis,
lau - dis of - fe - ri - mus: tu su - sci - pe pro a - ni - ma - bus il - lis,
lau - dis of - fe - ri - mus: tu su - sci - pe pro a - ni - ma - bus il - lis,

140

*) Takt 52, Instrumentalbaß, 2. Note: Süßmayr schreibt g.

55 Andante con moto

142

*) Takt 60, Viola, 6. Note: Süßmayr schreibt b.

63
Fag. I, II
a 2
A - brahae pro - mi - si - sti, pro - mi - si - sti,
pro - mi - si - sti, et se-mi-ni e - jus, quam o-lim A - brahae,
quam o-lim A - brahae pro - mi - si - sti, quam o-lim
et se-mi-ni e - jus,
Tutti Bassi

144

et se-mi-ni e - jus, quam o-lim A - brahae pro - mi-
et se-mi-ni e - jus, pro - mi - si - sti, quam o-lim A - brahae pro - mi-
A - brahae pro - mi - si - sti, quam o-lim A - brahae, quam o-lim A - brahae pro - mi-
et se-mi-ni e - jus, quam o-lim A - brahae pro - mi - si - sti,

*) Takt 71, Alt. 2. Takthälfte: Rhythmisierung bei Mozart

75
pro - mi - si - sti, et se - - mi-ni e - jus, et se - - mi-ni e - -
A - brahae pro - mi - si - sti, et se - mi-ni e - jus, et se - -
A - brahae pro - mi - si - sti, et se - mi-ni e - jus, et se -
A - brahae pro - mi - si - sti, et se - mi-ni e - jus, et se -

*) Takt 83 ff., Orgel: Bezifferung nach dem Stimmenerstdruck; vgl. Vorwort, S. XX, und Krit. Bericht.

148

si - sti, quam o-lim Abrahae promi - si - -sti, et se - - mi-ni e - -jus.
si - sti, quam o-lim Abrahae promi - si - -sti, et se - mi-ni, se-mi-ni e - -jus.
si - sti, quam o-lim Abrahae promi - si - -sti, et se - mi-ni, se-mi-ni e - -jus.
quam o-lim A-brahae promi - si-sti, promi - si - -sti, et se - mi-ni, se-mi-ni e - -jus.